PROFUSION AND DISORDER

A Book of Poetry

GEOFFREY EYRE

Mardle Publications

Also written by Geoffrey Eyre

A Plain Village
ISBN 978-0-9554608-1-4

Nutwhistle Farm
ISBN 978-0-9554608-2-1

The Poaching Gang
ISBN 978-0-9554608-3-8

The Case for Edward de Vere as Shakespeare
ISBN 978-0-9554608-4-5

Curlywigs
ISBN 978-0-9554608-5-2

Harpsichord Island
ISBN 978-0-9554608-6-9

Profusion & Disorder

Published by Mardle Publications

www.mardlepublications.com

mardlebooks@gmail.com

© 2015 Geoffrey Eyre

Typeset by John Owen Smith, Headley Down

All rights reserved. No part of this publication may be reproduced or transmitted in any material form, either electronically, mechanically, or by photocopying without prior permission of the copyright owner, all of the foregoing being in accordance with the UK Copyright, Designs and Patents Act 1998.

ISBN 978-0-9554608-7-6

Printed by CreateSpace

PROFUSION AND DISORDER

List of Poems

Profusion and Disorder	7
Transience	8
Washing Day	9
Coastguard Cottage	10
Orkney Sky at Night	11
Shrubs	12
Why Us?	13
The Sixth Extinction	14
Our Lonely Planet	16
Gravity	17
How Will It End?	18
Desecration	19
Heartbreak Planet	20
Our Wounded Planet	21
Volcano	22
Life Goes On	22
Wind and Fire	23
Building Site	24
Time	25
Quid Pro Quo	25
Cheery Chirrup	26
In Praise of Farmers	27
Autumn	28
Salesperson's Lament	29
Traveller Tales	30
Don't Intrude	31
History on the Big Screen	32
Hannibal ad Portas	33
No To Elections	34
In Praise of Politicians	35
William the Conqueror	36

The Dreaded 'S' Word	37
Ora Pro Nobis	38
Options	39
The Awkward Squad	40
Poverty, Piety, Wisdom and Freedom	41
Clockwork Mouse	42
The Many Deaths of a Champion	43
Transgression	44
Good Deed	44
Man of Principle	45
Back Benchers	45
Men Best Avoided	46
Second Thoughts	48
Drowned Woman	49
Lamplight	50
Lost Love	51
The River Stour : Summer afternoon	52
The River Stour : Winter midnight	53
Lingerie	54
Sweet Sorrow	54
First Kiss	55
Golden Wedding	56
Up Close and Personal	58
Love Cries Out	59
Love and Toothache	60
Fidelity	60
Love Won't Wait	61
Infidelity	61
Intensive Care	62
Motorcyclist in a Coma	63
Hotel Window	64
Unknown City	65
Hawk	66
Courage	67
Road Rage	68
Night Drive in a Big New Mercedes	70
Dreams	71

In Praise of Motorways	72
High Heels	73
Oil	74
Dirty Hands	75
Work and Prayer	76
Salisbury Cathedral	77
Heaven's Gate	78
Saints and Sinners	78
HIV Positive	79
Flu	80
Alzheimers	81
Losing Battle	81
The Sped Arrow	82
Our Lives in Their Hands	82
Death on the Table	83
Medical Dictionary	84
Mid Life Crisis	86
Epitaph Day	86
Carnal Pleasures	87
The Nipper	88
Ideas	89
K516	90
Hammerklavier	91
Making Hay	92
Don't Give Up The Day Job	93
Made Redundant	93
Mind Body and Soul	94
Always the Way	94
Probus Man	95
Three Magic Words	95
My Friend Ralph	96
Horoscope	96
Love Me, Love My Dog	97
Gift Wrapped	97
Unhandy Handyman	98
Unskilled Labour	99
Take a Bow	100

PROFUSION AND DISORDER

A tidy garden is not my idea of a garden.

Because nature is not tidy
nature is by nature prodigal
abundant, disorderly and profligate.
Flowers should not grow meekly in rows
they should bond in common purpose
flourish in clusters and clumps
jostle for their share of the light
for air, water and the right to expand
to flaunt their foliage, stems and blossoms
provide great swags of colour
filling every space in the flower border
plugging every gap in the vegetable patch
smothering paths with creeping jenny
walls with tumbling aubretia
allowing defiant weeds and rampant shrubs
to join forces and riot out of control.
All are welcome in my inclusive garden
where colours clash, bushes collide
and all is profusion and disorder.

Flowers ravish the eye and lift the spirit.
A summer garden bursting at the seams
resembles a pregnancy at full term
and sufficiently nurtured will deliver
hope, comfort and inspiration
to those who toil and blister
in its maintenance, plying the can
to provide tub-warmed rainwater
or ply the hoe to discourage intruders.
Not that weeds are always your enemy.
They serve a purpose and if doing no harm
should be allowed to stay
as should the snail on the thorn
and others of God's creatures
who treat our gardens as their own.

Lawns are not truly lawns
until trampled by pets and children
nor should you begrudge birds their fill
or deny them nesting space.
Sunshine and bird music come free
so make welcome all winged creatures
yes, even the dreaded Cabbage White
and in return the dragon-fly will reward you
with its skimming iridescent presence
and at scented dusk and stilly morn
all will be well with you and yours.

TRANSIENCE

A lazy drift of bonfire smoke
in upward wreaths and spirals
dissolves away into thin air
gone nowhere but gone for ever.

What of our memories
our precious remembrances
of times past, unique to us?
Do they also go up in smoke
do they too vanish into thin air
as fleeting as shadows
or rosebud dew in summer sun?

If so it is a humbling thought
that our busy lives
so full of purpose
so full of hope
leave little more behind
than breath on a mirror
or smoke from a bonfire.

WASHING DAY

My mother loved the wind.
She said a good stiff breeze
cured headaches
blew away the cobwebs
freshened things up
aired the house
and made all well.

To hear windows rattle
and watch sheets flap
cheered her up no end.
On washing days
she had a full line of whites
billowing like Nelson's fleet
under full sail.

Most of all my mother loved
a boisterous sou-wester
even when holding her hat on.
Loved to pile up autumn leaves
then scatter them with a kick.
Loved to laugh and run
with wind-reddened cheeks.

But she did not love the east wind.
She said it brought the plague
and other nasty diseases
from far-off lands across the sea.
Lands she had never seen
and never wished to see
if all she heard about them was true.

COASTGUARD COTTAGE

I was born in this isolated seashore cottage
I now own it, and I intend to die here.
I have kept it as it was, just as my mother
and my coastguard father would have known it.
The same solid door, the same clanking latch
and smell of stone floors and time-trapped dust
the same cliff path on which my school boots
scraped and slithered
the same clean salty sea-weedy seashore smell
I will delight in until I take my final breath.

Not forgetting the sea, the heavy pounding sea
beside which I have lived my life
never still, never silent, always menacing.
It is my first sight on waking
my last sight before sleeping
blue, grey, lime green, ever changing.
All day I hear the slap of water on rock
and the hiss of waves retreating through shingle
look out at the collapsing arcs of spray
rainbowed droplets sparkling in backlit sun.

I sail my boat and I go fishing
so I am close to the sea, the heavy pounding sea
and the creatures that therein dwell.
Wheeling squadrons of seagulls
serenade my waking hours
in a noisy and never-ending quest for food.
I watch them glide the dizzy midway air
winging and circling the clifftop breezes
where they scream in piercing angry stabs of sound
because no one loves gulls and life is hard.

A gunmetal sky presages a storm.
When angry purple clouds bestride the bay
the sea rises up and giant wave crests
thunder on the shingle below my window.
At night I imagine myself on board
a luckless freighter about to founder
with all hands in a black howling gale.
Wind rocks the cottage on its foundations
as though to wrench it from the ground
whirling me up, then down, into the waiting sea.

But things soon return to normal again.
I am a recluse and live my life in peace.
I love the running tide and the winter wind
that stings my face and waters my eyes
just as I love the white summer clouds
and my companionable fire at night
a driftwood fire that burns with a blue salty flame.
But most of all I love the sea itself
the ever-restless. cruel and heavy pounding sea
that will one day engulf us all.

ORKNEY SKY AT NIGHT

Go north if you want to see
a night sky dizzy with stars.
Stand on a distant shore
watch the stars dip into the sea
listen to the ocean's roar
feel the earth move and turn
know that you are standing
on a slowly spinning world
borne along in empty space.
Our sun a tiny twinkle
in someone else's night sky.

SHRUBS

You will regret buying a shrub.

Purchased to fill a gap
carried home in a tiny pot
planted in a dark corner
then forgotten
forever neglected and unloved
the life story of all shrubs.
But did it wither and die?
Was it composted? Bonfired?
None of the above
because shrubs are indestructible.
Laurels and the dreaded leylandii
march like conquerors across the land
and nothing short of an earthquake
or a hydrogen bomb
will rein in their rapid growth
or their unbridled lust for Lebensraum.
As commanded by their genetic profile
namely to expand in all directions
upwards, outwards and sideways
and finally to surge out of control
in revenge for your earlier neglect.
Their ground coverage is total
nothing else will grow for miles around
allowing them to swarm over paths
deprive your flower beds of light
while providing shelter to brambles
of the glove-penetrating thorniest variety.
Shrubs are a gardening nightmare without end
resistant as saddle leather and high tensile steel
they will defy your puny efforts
to restrain them with saw and loppers.
Instead they conspire with adjacent shrubs
to form an impenetrable hostile jungle
provide habitat for pernicious wild life
and undermine the foundations of your house.

You cannot fight shrubs and win
so accept defeat with good grace
hasten to the nearest estate agent
and make it someone else's problem.

WHY US?

How did anything so intricate, so wonderful
as the human body come to exist
on this most unassuming of planets
in a far distant corner of so vast a universe.

And not just to exist but to thrive and flourish
obeying the summons to go forth and multiply
to people the planet in wealth and diversity
and refashion it to our needs in great cities.

Why does the human body go wrong so rarely?
Most of us are sane and healthy most of the time
and many are creative. Which other world
can boast its Mozart, its Michelangelo?

Once upright on two legs the rise of humankind
was unstoppable and still marches on
to the sound of sackbuts and cornets
in one long unending spectacular triumph.

Why us? It is the greatest of all mysteries.

THE SIXTH EXTINCTION

The Sixth Extinction is coming along nicely
if our mad scientists are to be believed.
Do they mean us? They surely do.
Proud Man, the enemy of all
is long overdue for his punishment
not in vengeance by Planet Earth
but from so many self-inflicted wounds.

Since recovering from the Fifth Extinction
when perished the dinosaurs
it is now our turn to be snuffed out
an extermination we thoroughly deserve.
Because we have indeed brought it on ourselves
not only in past desecrations of the planet
but in the pollution of the Here and Now.

Eruptions and inundations, unfriendly impacts
and acidification, spaced over four billion years
led to Extinctions One, Two, Three and Four.
Inconvenient but ultimately recoverable
because Mother Earth survived, Nature adapted
and life, however primitive, however precarious,
clawed its way back over millions of years.

Now that we are launched into the Sixth Extinction
all our beautiful wild animals are vulnerable.
The genera of terrestrial and marine life
will succumb species by species
until it will be only rats, cockroaches and us
competing for an ever-dwindling supply
of food and water, warmth and shelter.

From Day One of the Industrial Revolution
we sowed the sooty seeds of our destruction.
The foundries and machinery of wealth creation
served also as the instruments of our ruin
setting in motion the inexorable sequence of events
that will rob us of breathable air and drinkable water
poison our oceans and darken out the sun.

'Anoxia' is the word to remember
and even if it does not frighten the cavalry
it should certainly frighten you.
Because, my friend, this dread word
signals the kiss of death for Humankind.
Absence of Oxygen is what Anoxia means
and without precious life-sustaining Oxygen we die.

In the Gas Wars, now gathering momentum
Carbon Dioxide is assured of victory
and Oxygen of defeat, a dismal prospect.
Because when Carbon Dioxide wins we lose.
The oceans are turned to blood
forests become deserts, rivers run dry
and the world as we love it and desecrate it, ends.

So we too must adapt, in the fond hope
that human brainpower and endurance
will rescue us from the pickle we are in.
Let us hope that lessons will be learned
and action taken to reverse the damage
or at least to slow down the rapid rate
at which Humankind is hurtling to its doom.

OUR LONELY PLANET

Why do our mad scientists love space so much?
Astrophysicists from around the world
offer us enlightenment through algebra
to explain the irradiated horror and emptiness
which surrounds our vulnerable planet.
They gesticulate excitedly at display boards
filled top to bottom with meaningless squiggles
then baffle us with their superior knowledge
every day some new theory of how it all began.

Astronomy makes riveting television.
We lounge in comfort and watch worlds collide
witness stars at the instant of their creation
munch popcorn while other stars die
supernovas that perish in starburst glory
galaxies that implode into fathomless black holes
a cosmic fireworks display that defies logic
quintillions of years back into the past
of our violent, chaotic and hostile universe.

Is space real? Or is it just twinkling lights
glimpsed through pinpricks in a dark canopy?
Is there any hope of escape from our doomed planet?
Can we relocate to a more benign part of the cosmos?
Any sent message would take many human lifetimes
to arrive, and many more still to await the reply
so we must face the fact that our tiny planet
a microdot in the endless void, is out of range
leaving us to fend for ourselves as best we can.

A sobering thought.

GRAVITY

For every action there is an equal
and opposite reaction.
Thus spake God's agent on earth
Sir Isaac Newton. A man who knew
what he was talking about
even though he wrote it in Latin
for our better understanding.
Actioni contrarium semper
et aequalem esse reactionem.

The great man knew better than most
what makes the world go round.
He studied the Sun and the Moon
where the hours and the centuries
pass as one, ageing us as they go.
He worked out how it is done
how they keep time and distance
one from another. He called it
his Third Law of Motion.

Gravity is the engine which powers
this celestial clock ticking life away
in the unending dance of time.
The patterned hieroglyphs
are printed in advance, we merely
go through Newton's Motions.
Morning progresses to afternoon
then day to night, summer to winter,
youth to age. And finally life to death.

O quam cito transit gloria mundi

HOW WILL IT END?

Our stricken planet is time expired
and one day the furnace below our feet
will lurch out of control and trigger the implosion
programmed into all celestial bodies
as their showy farewell to the universe.
Apocalypse now? Yes, my friend, it is
and you are right to be alarmed as you read this.
Our shining sea cities are all vulnerable
sited at the confluence of rivers and oceans
which co-exist in an uneasy compromise
the eternal contention between wind and tide
to determine which is the stronger.

What next? We are all afraid of the dark
and need to be reassured that at the end
all will be well with the well-intentioned.
Religionists do their best to comfort us
and we must be grateful to them for that
although I doubt they have the answers we seek.
And even if there is a place for departed souls
the chances of finding it with a spacecraft
are not great, one would suspect.
So what to do? Make the best of what we have
take better care of our beleaguered planet
and pray for the future of our grandchildren.

DESECRATION

O God, what have we done?
What have we done to your wonderful world
the world you created in seven days.
In seven days a whole world?
Incredible!
You got a move on God
and deserve our thanks
our most sincere and heartfelt thanks
for providing us with this wonderful world
this generous world of plenty
so swiftly conjured from rock and fire
for our labour and delight
and which we have so thoroughly trashed.

O God, why are you silent?
Why are you not vengeful?
Why do you not condemn and reproach us?
Where is your wrath?
Your righteous anger?
Your scorn?
You would be justified, well and truly justified
to visit a pestilence upon us
to punish us with Old Testament fury
for the desecration of your beautiful planet
so lovingly fashioned in seven days
for our labour and delight
and which we have so thoroughly trashed.

HEARTBREAK PLANET

I like this planet, God said
It's got possibilities
So I'll give them a start

With Eve newlywed
A figleaf for her chemise
Wedding march by Mozart

To air her marriage bed
Not in the Outer Hebrides
Or some other distant part

But in the sunny Med
Fanned with a spicy breeze
To give love a kick-start

A Garden, a flowerbed
And nothing to displease
Eve and her sweetheart

Eve comes to childbed
Mother of the seven seas
As the tribes fly apart

We're on our way, God said
It's ten of the best for these
My children, laws to impart

Better they should be in dread
Of me than Mephistopheles
That smooth-talking upstart

Keep the faith or be misled
Because the origin of species
Favours Darwin over Descartes

Others opt for Marx instead
Money doesn't grow on trees
Working hard is just not smart.

Too soon the nuclear warhead
Whole nations on their knees
And propaganda the blackest art

Much blood will be shed
So many enemies to appease
And we all end in the dustcart

It's a crying shame, God said.
Even for one of my expertise
This planet breaks my heart.

OUR WOUNDED PLANET

Earthquakes and erupting volcanoes are bad news.
They are violent, they are dangerous
and happen much too often
on our fragile and increasingly polluted planet.
There is a fiery furnace below our feet
the source of all these random irruptions
in our earth's unstable and irritable bowels.
Earthquakes and volcanoes are capricious.
They cause havoc but also serve a purpose.
They are our wounded planet's way
of drawing to our attention that all is not well
with our governance of Mother Earth.

VOLCANO

A crater blasting out ash and molten rock
is not easily ignored
the glowing lava flow a fearful sight
as all in its path is instantly devoured
consumed in cindered sacrifice
to the sulphurous netherworld below.

Smoke, fumes and ash blot out the sun
our precious life sustaining sun
turns summers to winter
lays waste to the oceans
and provides artists with lurid sunsets
to paint in Post-Impressionist abandon.

LIFE GOES ON

The life force comes embedded in our loins
our contribution and responsibility
to the evolutionary process.
Our seed, our eggs
ensure more than mere survival
they confer advancement
learning, accomplishment, joy and beauty
and the facility for bequeathing knowledge
because even the least gifted of parents
can produce children of talent.
How exalted to bring a dancer into the world
a mathematician, an engineer or a poet.

Through our children we live again, and for ever.

WIND AND FIRE

A barn fire
bales of hay and straw
valuable winter feed destroyed in half an hour

We watch, helpless
shivering in a cold wind
with few to witness on a bleak January midnight

The wind is from the east
dry and icy, viciously penetrating
fanning the flames like the bellows of a forge

We watch, awed
by this primal force of nature
its destructive momentum completely unstoppable

Wind and fire
nothing can resist them
when they team up to destroy something

A blood red furnace
streams of wind-driven sparks
and a voracious angry roar as if mad with hunger

A big fire is truly fearsome
generating a ferocious internal energy
from the humble ingredients it so eagerly devours

Our barn fire serves as a warning
a harsh reminder that the weapons of nature
fire, wind and flood, are elemental and all-powerful.

BUILDING SITE

You have to admire them, the ground levellers
their lives bounded in mud
mud, chaos and constant noise
urged on by the thump of pile drivers
and the throaty roar of diesel engines
as bulldozers and dumper trucks
churn up the muddy battlefield
while excavators carve ready-mix channels
so that order may be created from disorder.

Hard hats and steel-tipped boots
are de rigueur for the groundwork men
impervious to drenching rain
buffeting wind or searing heat.
When the solid foundations have been laid
what then? They repeat the process elsewhere
leaving others to lay the first brick
raise the scaffold poles
and magic the new building into life.

This the levellers never see
the finished product of their labour
theirs only the empty plot and the first sod
the clamour of machines
and lives spent making way for others.
For consolation consider this
the Parthenon, the Doge's Palace
Salisbury Cathedral, Versailles and the Shard
all started life as building sites.

TIME

Why do the young have so much
of this precious commodity
when the rest of us have so little?
Only they can afford to waste it
because to squander time
is worse folly than wasting money.

Those who visit the sick
read to their children
or comfort the lonely
are the only true givers
because time is worth more
than all the money ever coined.

Nor can time be traded.
Money can buy everything else
but the angel of death
with bony beckoning finger
cannot be bribed for extra time
when the whistle sounds for us.

Do not look round as you read this.
The unpleasant noise you hear
is that thieving bastard Time
gurgling down the plug-hole
of all our yesterdays
and most of our tomorrows.

QUID PRO QUO

Has it ever occurred to you
that even undertakers die
and need someone else
to bury them?

CHEERY CHIRRUP

Eyeing me bleakly
from a mildewed apple tree
dripping with winter rain
a bird.

It held on for dear life
watching me with suspicion
deep suspicion
even though I meant it no harm.

A starveling thrush
perched on a topmost twig
huddled, ruffled, miserable
and past caring.

It had survived the night
but saw no good reason
to herald the dawn
with a cheery chirrup.

A mournful stave
was all it could manage
by way of hoarse song
and grudging thanks.

A bedraggled spotty fowl
with no ambition left
except to see out the day
and guard its territory.

It had killed its parents
driven out siblings and cousins
to acquire Lebensraum
and first go with the worms.

My garden its kingdom
Lord of all it surveyed
from its mildewed twig
on a rain-sodden apple tree.

Secure in the knowledge
that birds were here first
and will still be here
long after we have perished.

IN PRAISE OF FARMERS

Farms are special places.
Nothing grows on its own
not even grass.
Cows do not give milk
we take it from them
without their consent.
The seed, the harvest
and the new-born lamb
are endless miracles
of rebirth and renewal.
Only unremitting daily toil
can extricate order
from the chaos of nature
and produce useful things
for us to eat, drink, use and wear.
Farmers by this definition
are special people
greatly to be admired.

AUTUMN

How I hate the Autumn
that interminable drab
chill apology for a season.

The Spring, now that
is a different matter.
After Spring cometh
beautiful Summer.
It may be only fleeting
it is unlikely to be fine
but never mind.
Summer is Summer
everything grows
and the sun shines.

Not for long though.
Shadows lengthen
flowers droop and die
and dreary Autumn
returns all too soon.
How I seethe with fury
when kindly folk
who should know better
exclaim about the leaf fall
with its rich colouring
enthuse at mellow warmth
in this ruin of the year
when all I see is decay
and the countryside
is one long squelch.

After which comes
black December
a mournful bugle blast
to herald the season
sent to punish us
for our manifold
sins and wickedness.

Dear God, how I hate
horrible Winter
even more than I
loathe and detest
Christmas.
Just the thought
of ice, frost and snow
rings a savage bell clang
that does my head
no good at all.
How I abominate
the cold and dark.
How I long for the sun
for light and warmth
when cats stretch out
and women's legs
go bare again.

No more invective
it is bad for my soul
as well as my digestion.
A heartfelt plea instead.
Why can we not have
two seasons instead of four?
Two are all we need.
Lovely pregnant Spring
burgeoning Summer
then back to Spring again.

God, are you listening to me?

SALESPERSON'S LAMENT

Winning a new account
although good
is not as good
as losing an old one is bad.

TRAVELLER TALES

Travel was not always easy.
Pilgrims sought safety in numbers
guided tours from shrine to shrine
medieval package holidays for the pious
some on foot, some on donkeys
and some on crutches
but all brimmed with faith
hoping for the reward of the godly
their seat in heaven booked.

Travel may have been slow
it may have been dangerous
but it was also exciting
and young men seeking adventure
or fleeing jurisdiction
took the shilling, wore the uniform
joined the army and saw the world
at the government's expense.
Their graves circle the globe.

Traveller tales are tall tales
of winged horses and seven league boots
that whizz you around the planet
without saddle sores or foot blisters.
No weary plod over plains and mountains
and no need to pay for a ticket.
Is it a bird? Is it a plane?
No, it is the human imagination
taking off on a broomstick.

Flying horses are too slow
for the modern man in a hurry
flitting between galaxies
dodging back and forth in time
by dint of super-speed teleportation.
Here on Mother Earth one minute
reassembled atom by atom
quintillions of miles away the next.
It's all so easy on a TV screen!

Vicariously is the best way to travel
an armchair in a cosy room
book on knee and drink to hand
reading of hardships endured
and indignities suffered
sharing the pain by proxy
in a well-written travel book.
Not only less arduous
but so much cheaper too!

Whether frostbitten at the ice caps
dangling from mountain ropes
eaten alive by insects in jungle swamps
dying of thirst in blistering deserts
adrift in shark infested seas
buried in an avalanche
captured by hostile tribesmen
or held hostage by religious zealots
we applaud their literary efforts.

Yes, sooner you than us, mate
but thanks for taking the trouble
to let us know what it was like
and what you are planning
for your next adventure
sanity and broken bones permitting.
Travel broadens the mind
or it should, and travellers' tall tales
are always worth the telling.

DON'T INTRUDE

Children holding hands
dance round and round
in a playground game
only children know
and only children
need to know.

HISTORY ON THE BIG SCREEN

Revisionist history is the best history
so let's hear it for the film makers
that band of bold warrior directors
and strutting square-jawed thesps
who won us two World Wars.
Tanned, toned and sleekly groomed
with parade-ground snappy salutes
and steely quarterdeck gaze
they rewrote the history of conflict
and made it better. Why not?
Enemies bite the dirt, the good guys win
seems like a bright idea to me.

A camera crew is all you need
a little nerve, an imaginative script
some judiciously applied pressure
to the backside of circumstance
and lo! We won that war after all.
The shadow trumps the substance
with Truth as always the first casualty.
It bleeds on the cutting room floor
while the marzipan foot soldiers
of the great Motion Picture Regiment
march forth to fight the good fight
by proxy on our behalf.

HANNIBAL AD PORTAS

Panic and rumour in Ancient Rome
Hannibal is at the gates!

He wasn't, but we know the feeling
because there is always someone
somewhere, willing to frighten us.
It may not be Hannibal
but our enemies are still at the gates.
We cannot see them but we fear them
and cower like children in the dark.

Radio telescopes and spy satellites
sweep the empty air
for tiny squiggles of hostile sound.
These contraptions and others like them
not angels, watch over us by day
and read our minds by night.
Paranoia rules, and it's not okay.

What have we to fear that is worse
than the fear we inflict on ourselves?
Are we safer? Are we more free?
Happier? Wiser? Better informed?
The Thought Police have your number
my friend, so download at your peril
anything titillating, or worse, subversive.

Watchman, what of the night?
These days it's better not to ask.

NO TO ELECTIONS

Our precious liberties
hard won over centuries
we owe not to democracy
but to secularism.

Democracy is divisive
and making aid dependent
on holding elections
votes in those we like least.

Elections open old wounds
old scores are settled
tribal loyalties prevail
and nothing changes.

Secularism is not democracy
even if media pundits
who ought to know better
pontificate as though it was.

How exalted to be free!
Long live secularism
and strong institutions
the guardians of our liberty.

IN PRAISE OF POLITICIANS

Of what use is an alpha male
if not to serve his community?
High self esteem, the gift of the gab, conceit in
overplus
are commodities in short supply
and should be placed at the disposal
of those of us who are not vain
do not speak easily in public
but are timid and humble and know our place.

We need bold foresters to keep the wolves at bay
so step forward gentlemen of high ambition and thick
skin
and ladies similarly endowed and inclined.
We invite you to preen before us at the hustings
parade your venality, emote with eye-watering
insincerity
the stock-in-trade of politicians the world over.
What are lies to the gullible? We deserve to be lied to
just as there are truths we do not want to hear.

Because we love our acorn-brained politicos
who brag and cheat and fornicate and lie
knowing we have the least worst system of governance
ever invented. Would we like any better a junta?
A kleptocracy? Or zealots of whatever stripe?
However rebarbative the scoundrels we elect
however egregious their parties or crass their leaders
we always end up with the politicians we deserve.

WILLIAM THE CONQUEROR

The hot topic of conversation
in the London pubs and clubs of 1066
was much the same as now – Europe.
To join or not to join
and once in, whether to stay in.
These were the questions
exercising the minds of those with most to lose.

Step forward William the Bastard
Duke of Normandy and boat burner
who settled the matter by force of arms
arriving in London by way of Pevensey Bay
and the Battle of Hastings
then crowned in the Abbey on Christmas Day
as our newly anointed king and sovereign lord.

King William allowed no challenge to his authority
seeing it as divinely sanctioned and approved
so the debate over Europe
whether to be in or out, was thus decided for us
by armed invasion and defeat
a regime change not much to our liking
but remains to this day a hot topic of conversation.

William the Bastard was not a very nice man
but we owe a debt of gratitude
to this dour and mighty prince
who by force of character
as much as by force of arms
hammered the native British, that means us,
first into submission and then into shape.

THE DREADED 'S' WORD

Socialism is the noblest cause
the most altruistic, the most lofty
the purest and best-intentioned
of all political philosophies.
Men and women of the left
do not neglect the S word
I beseech and implore you.
It has become the creed
that dare not speak its name.
Neither Shop Floor nor High Table
any longer sing of Jerusalem
or the Red Flag beneath which
they were once proud to live and die
nor flaunt their pink credentials
in our property owning plutocracy.

Mention the brotherhood of man
and wince at the embarrassed silence
which greets this bad taste remark
in the wine bars of middle England.
Socialism is out of fashion
leaving the sincerely decent among us
with nowhere to donate our voting X.
Yet it remains the only ism
that places the welfare of little children
above the pride of princes
and for that very compelling reason
I commend the S word
to the slightly dotty, to the unworldly
and all my fellow idealists
who know a lost cause when we see one.

ORA PRO NOBIS

Please pray for the following

Pray for the permanently sick and the mentally ill
pray for the disabled in mind or body
pray for drunkards and drug addicts
pray for prostitutes and gamblers
pray for all those in prisons and institutions
pray for the senile and demented
pray for single parents and homeless teenagers
pray for the ignorant and uneducated
pray for the weak, the inadequate and the bullied
pray for the abused and the neglected
pray for the unemployed and the unemployable
pray for those without money
pray for those who will never have any money
pray for persecuted minorities
pray for the oppressed and the exploited
pray for the hungry
pray for the lonely
pray for the dying
pray for the godless, the weary and all those who weep.

The unseen multitude who still need our daily prayers in this richest of nations.

OPTIONS

Is it not
better to be loved than hated
better to be rich than poor
better to be healthy than sick
better to be happy than miserable
better to be kind than unkind
better to be comely than ugly
better to be generous than stingy
better to have friends than enemies
better to be smart than stupid
better to be busy than idle
better to be a giver than a receiver
better to give willingly than grudgingly
better to be honest than dishonest
better to be a lover than a lecher
better to be humble than too proud
better to be frugal than greedy
better to have a good name than be reviled
better to be admired than despised
better to be courteous than ill-mannered
better to be discreet than a blabbermouth
better to be tolerant than a bigot
better to be embarrassed than ashamed
better to be destitute than demeaned
better to be cursed than pitied
better to suffer an injustice than commit a crime
better to die on your feet than live on your knees
better to be in a grave than dependent on others
better to be anything than old and lonely.

THE AWKWARD SQUAD

I do not like people who smile
I distrust them instinctively.
It is not natural to smile.
I do not smile myself
and do not expect or wish
anyone to smile at me.

I do not like beautiful people
I distrust them instinctively.
Beautiful people smile a lot
having much to smile about.
I am not beautiful myself
so I dislike beautiful people.

I do not like rich people
I distrust them instinctively.
The poor are always with us
so unfortunately are the rich.
I am not rich myself
so I dislike rich people.

Long live the Awkward Squad
them I like, and mostly trust.
They may not be beautiful
they may not smile much
and they are seldom rich.
Instead they have principles.

You cannot bribe or buy
still less intimidate
a genuine paid-up member
of the Awkward Squad.
To join this select band
is my dearest ambition.

They fly the rallying flag
for those of us to whom
smiling does not come easily
are neither rich nor beautiful
but who are just naturally
obtuse and bloody-minded.

POVERTY, PIETY, WISDOM AND FREEDOM

No one can help being poor
but poverty is not liberating
just as wisdom makes you
neither rich, nor free.
Money can buy most things
but wisdom is not one of them.
Wisdom is a heartbreaker
that brings certain sorrow
since the more you know
the harder life is to bear.
The pious are seldom wise,
seldom rich, and rarely free.
Only the ignorant are truly poor
Only the scholar is truly free.

CLOCKWORK MOUSE

We come into the world ready-packaged
hardwired with a coiled spring
a tightly wound
and individually tensioned spring
to power us safely through
the ups and downs and ins and outs
of life's long journey
our three score years and ten.

Then scurry about like clockwork mice
hither, thither, sideways and backwards
mostly getting nowhere.
At the end of our allotted span
questions may legitimately be asked.
How tightly wound was your spring?
How tightly wound was mine?
Was it a rehearsal or the real thing?

Either way the same result.
With no kind celestial hand to turn the key
and wind us up for a second go round
we are put back into the toy cupboard
not so much broken or discarded
as time expired
our spring finally run down
our fragile mechanism conked out.

Just one more clockwork mouse
that ran its course
and then was seen and heard no more.

THE MANY DEATHS OF A CHAMPION

We see it in their haunted eyes
heavy with apprehension as they face defeat
knowing the cavernous emptiness that awaits
when triumphs cease and glory fades.

The new champion's arms are raised
and the old champion must quit the stage
with an utterance many times rehearsed
a few gracious words through gritted teeth.

But not yet. Not quite yet.

Because once more the old champion wins
grinding out a victory against the odds
brain and sinew long past breaking point
but fuelled in equal desperation
by pride, anger, jealousy and fear
the fateful day is one more time deferred.

Such hard-fought victories come at a cost
in pain, suffering and the foretaste of death
which must be many times endured
until that day comes, as it surely will
when the coup de grâce is finally delivered
and the long emptiness begins.

TRANSGRESSION

An upright man of faith, any faith
is a man greatly to be admired.
The straight and narrow is a hard path to travel
uphill all the way and then some.
Faith is so fragile when put to the test
temptation as hard to avoid as it is to resist
because the devil not only has the best tunes
but the most persuasive arguments
and the most seductive advertising.

An upright man of faith might be forgiven
if every once in a while he stumbles
and succumbs to the pleasures of the flesh
or the bottle, the racetrack or the casino
the lure of easy money and not being caught
propelled just as we are in our ignorance
by greed or lust or fear. What to do?
We would forgive him his transgression
but would he ever forgive himself?

GOOD DEED

Sometimes the good you do
does you no good at all.

Do someone a favour
and make an enemy for life.

Did you expect gratitude?
That's not how it works.

No good deed ever goes unpunished.

MAN OF PRINCIPLE

Being a man of principle is all very well
but between principle and obstinacy
the line is finely drawn.
To hurt or not to hurt? That is the dilemma.
The rigid man who cannot or will not bend
but is nevertheless willing to hurt his friend
for fear of showing weakness
or worse, betraying his principles
will sacrifice happiness, career, life itself
sooner than trim and give a little
concede a point here and there
and settle for second best in an argument.

Principles have merit, but come with a price.

BACKBENCHERS

How I love to see all those
stony-faced backbenchers
arms folded in disapproval
at the focus-group chicanery
and mendacious spin-doctoring
perpetrated in their name.
Shop stewards and shiresmen
they sit foursquare in the light
beyond the penumbra of venality.
Despised by the party bigwigs
derided by press and media
laud them, ye humble subjects
of the Crown. Laud them.
The protectors of all our liberties.

MEN BEST AVOIDED

Advice from a maiden aunt.

On no account, my aunt said
trust a man wearing jewellery.
One ring I wouldn't like
but could just about tolerate.
Two or more indicates a pervert
a scoundrel or an adulterer
pick and mix them how you will.
A blazer I can just about stomach
with a bow tie or a cravat, never!
As for beards, my aunt said
be warned. Beards are bad news.
Never trust a man with a beard.

But Aunt, I replied, times change.
Most of the men who ask me out
although unbearded, are whiskery.
It's called designer stubble.

Don't argue with me, girl,
my aunt said. I know what
I'm talking about. Men should
stand closer to the razor
if they want my respect.
Remember my words, child.
Men who wear male perfume
not only smell dreadful
but are up to no good.
Men who take you by the elbow
should be kicked good and hard
where it hurts most.
Furthermore, my aunt said,

never trust a man whose eyes
are too close together.
A rogue, no doubt about it.

But Aunt, I replied
even if a man knew that his eyes
were too close together
and regretted same
his opportunities for rectifying
the condition are somewhat limited
wouldn't you agree?

I haven't finished, my aunt said.
Avoid like the plague men who boast
of rich friends or titled relations.
Men in tight jeans are more interested
in their ass than yours. Take heed and
learn from one who has delved deep
into the world's deceit and trickery.
Men who gaze into your eyes
and speak words of love
want only to get into your knickers
with or without your consent
and at the earliest opportunity.
Be in no doubt of their insincerity.
Nor trust a man with a limp handshake
my aunt continued, speaking earnestly.
Pay attention. Delete immediately
from your list of prospective suitors
any man who eats sweets, acts in plays,
keeps his money in a purse,
has a foreign sounding name
or worse, an accent you can't place.
Men who whistle while they work
should be fed bird seed until they stop.

Men who wear berets are always odd
but no odder than old men in shorts.
Her lecture concluded my maiden aunt
allowed herself a modest boast.
I have treasured my virginity
as if it were a pearl beyond price.
Do likewise, Liebchen,
and a long and happy life will be yours.

I guess my aunt does not like men
very much. Hardly at all, in fact.

SECOND THOUGHTS

My wimp of a husband had to go
he didn't fit the profile
for an independent modern woman
well able to make it on her own.
He cried like a baby
when I gave him his marching orders
but got no sympathy from me.
I was his wife for God's sake
not his mother.

But now that I am so much older
and live alone in a silent house
where everything I touch feels cold
I miss him, the soft-hearted sod.
He thought the world of me
and now I think of him
all the time remembering
how safe and warm it felt
when we slept together side by side.

DROWNED WOMAN

I bought in an auction
an antique mirror.
A cheval glass
French, if the catalogue
is to be believed.
Free standing on castors,
full length, swivelling.
A handsome piece.

The glass is silvered,
the reflection dark
and slightly wavering
as if looking into water.
When I approach
and loosen my hair
I see another woman
staring back at me.

A drowning woman
her hair like waterweed
curious eyes watching me
as I slowly remove my dress.
Moonlight pale as death
she slides silently down
into the translucent glass
and the peaceful water.

Who is the woman watching me
from this antique cheval glass
her hair like strands of weed
teased out by running water
her face as white as death?

Why does she haunt my mirror?
Does she see my face clearly?
Or darkly, as I see hers?
There is a river not far from here.
Perhaps I shall find the answer
if I kneel by that peaceful water.
Whose face will stare back at me
from beneath the waiting river?
Will it be mine or will it be hers?

I will go tonight and find out
which of us lives in the mirror.

LAMPLIGHT

Lamplight is for bus queues
the homeward bound
dog walkers, drunks
and lovers.

Of course, lovers, who else?
A pale dim yellow lamp
finely falling rain
and the first embrace.

Magic. Never forget
that lamplight moment
the upturned face
and the lingering lips.

A drizzly November night
is turned to gold
in the pale dim lamplight
when lovers kiss.

LOST LOVE

Visiting the haunts of past delight
where no one stands tonight again
under the pale dim yellow light.

Waiting, waiting, hope ever bright
to see your outline blurred in rain
visiting the haunts of past delight.

Our special place, as lovers, reunite
and fly together body, soul and brain
under the pale dim yellow light.

Waiting where no one stands in sight
void the penumbra, once more in vain
visiting the haunts of past delight.

To wait alone is love's dearest spite
a sad song with an old refrain
under the pale dim yellow light.

Empty half shadows, I quit the night
and rue lost love in lasting pain
visiting the haunts of past delight
under the pale dim yellow light.

THE RIVER STOUR

Summer afternoon

Beside the ever-brimming
slow and steady Dorset Stour
stands a pinnacled church
and on its tall spiked tower
glints in the sun a gilded clock
its sonorous clanking chime
tolling three in the afternoon
with few around to listen
on a day of shimmering heat
at the height of summer.
Sun muffled and languorous
it scarcely reaches to the cows
drowsing in the water meadows
or the skimming river birds.
A heavy and pleasant stillness
stifles the passage of time
in this timeless place
where the years and the hours
pass as one, and our children
grow old in their turn
beside the ever-brimming
slow and steady Dorset Stour.

THE RIVER STOUR

Winter midnight

Beside the ever-brimming
slow and steady Dorset Stour
stands a pinnacled church
and on its tall spiked tower
glints in the moonlight
a gilded clock.
Midnight cold and crystal clear
magnifies in the frozen air
each sonorous clanking stroke
the full slow midnight dozen
stacking up chime on chime
a breaking cadence of sound
to roll across the water meadows
before easing away downstream
echo by dying echo
through the frost-chilled silence
of a mist-rising river valley.
Prolonged and slowly fading
these echoes of innocence and regret
are for remembrance of times past
spent beside the ever-brimming
slow and steady Dorset Stour.

SWEET SORROW

What is sweeter
than lovers meeting?
What is sadder
than lovers parting?

Two questions
one easy answer
don't ask me
how I know.

Nothing is sweeter
than lovers meeting.
Nothing is sadder
than lovers parting.

LINGERIE

Why do men like black so much?
There has to be a reason.

Black for funerals
and black for the bedroom?

Social anthropologists please explain.

FIRST KISS

In all of life
there is no thrill
like the first embrace
of young lovers.

Nothing sweeter
than mingled breath
startled eyes
and the first kiss.

Keep it ever so.
Do not forget
how good it was
that first kiss.

Keep it tucked
in your back memory
to recall at will
when times are hard.

Whatever happens
keep that moment
safe and sacred.
It will never come again.

GOLDEN WEDDING

Fifty years ago the sun beamed down

on churchyard conker trees
spiked pink and white
with exotic candles of blossom
colour matched to the awning
and the pew-end posies
waiting to greet the bride.
On the church tower, a flag
across the village street, bunting.
Not so much a wedding
more of a village festival
to which everyone was invited
and expected to take part.
The lord of the manor's daughter
was marrying a young toff
in a posh Society wedding.
Hence the clustered paparazzi
and the rubberneckers jostling
for their first glimpse of the bride.

While they waited
the chimes of an opportunist ice-cream van
added a descant to the church bells.
A helmeted policeman, arms folded
leaned against his motorbike.
On the manor house lawn
case after case of champagne
disappeared into a giant marquee.
Smoked salmon sandwiches
arrived by the van-load.
Children romped
stray dogs arrived to join in the fun
and little girls and their grandmothers
skipped hand-in hand
to the sound of wedding music.

The ceremony over
an accolade of subalterns
with upraised swords
saluted the fortunate couple.
Bride shimmering white
husband in red with gold buttons
a flotilla of sailor-suited pageboys to their right
a froth of bridesmaids in pink to their left.

Now for a look at the guests
starting with the ladies.
Stunning gazelles in tailored suits
with fashionable short skirts
showed enough bronzed leg
to make old married men weep
hot tears of frustration and envy.
Their watchful mothers wore Liberty
and wide-brimmed elegant hats.
Their menfolk sported toppers
and cutaway coats.
As a wedding it was a very dressy affair.

Not forgetting the peasantry.
A border of apple-cheeked cottagers
oohed and aahed. A side aisle
of pensioners from the almshouses
remembered the bride from babyhood.
A squeal of Guides and Brownies
threw tissue-paper rose petals.
Sturdy tenant farmers in brown suits
accompanied by wives in print frocks
took things much more calmly
and looked forward to the eats.
An anthem of pretty choirboys
ruffed and red-gowned
drew their pay in the vestry.

A peal of shirtsleeved bell-ringers
having finished their stint
went to the pub.
A thirsty lot, bell-ringers.
And lastly, leaning over the pub wall
morosely supping from pint pots
a mulch of sour-faced old joskins
shook their grizzled heads
in stern and silent disapproval
at all the fuss and expense.

Convinced the marriage would never last.

UP CLOSE AND PERSONAL

Close encounters are fun
the closer the better
if you are making love

Close encounters are less fun
if you are making war
instead of making love

The clash of armies
brings little pleasure
to the likes of you and me

So cuddle up and be nice
to one another
while remembering this

No close encounter
will ever beat
a kiss.

LOVE CRIES OUT

Some things cannot be hidden

Big hands for one
big feet for another
nor can a cough
be long suppressed.
If you are poor
however hard you try
to pretend otherwise
no one is fooled.
Poverty cries out.
It cannot be hidden.

If you are in love
nothing you do
when you are together
goes unobserved.
If you think anyone
is fooled when you
pretend indifference
think again.
Love also cries out
and cannot be hidden.

LOVE AND TOOTHACHE

Just as toothache
makes you forget
a headache
so love drives
everything else
out of mind.

Sport, family,
friends, hobbies
all forgotten.
Love ruins
everything.
A bit of a sod, really.

FIDELITY

Fidelity
is out of fashion.
Serial adultery is all the go.

So why do I
stay true to you?
Could love have anything to do with it?

LOVE WON'T WAIT

Love comes
in all shapes
and sizes.

Do not refuse
any offer
of love.

Whenever it comes
however it comes
do not hesitate.

Accept at once
because love
is like that.

Love is impatient
and never waits
for anyone.

INFIDELITY

Heaven weeps when lovers part
for love is never what it seems
and nothing heals a broken heart.
Too late now to ask me why
so many hopes and dreams
vanished in the twinkling of a lie.

INTENSIVE CARE

My Spanish night nurse, silent, restless
Thin armed, unsmiling, dressed in white
Prowling and padding like a leopardess.

So many painful memories to suppress
Bearable only when I have in sight
My Spanish night nurse, silent, restless.

Bad dreams and dark shadows coalesce
Phantoms my night nurse puts to flight
Prowling and padding like a leopardess.

Back from the brink is a slow process
She leans over me at deep midnight
My Spanish night nurse, silent, restless.

She fingers my pulse with deft finesse
Inching me, inching me back into light
Prowling and padding like a leopardess.

Her cool hand I feel as a feathery caress
She is my guide as brain and body reunite
My Spanish night nurse, silent, restless
Prowling and padding like a leopardess.

MOTORCYCLIST IN A COMA

A mirrored hall far beyond sleep
a long hall, warm and very still
where a young man paces slowly
all need to hurry for ever gone.
It is a hall of memories and dreams
of half-remembered names and faces
of first loves and childhood friends
who watch from the walled mirrors
as he passes by in his timeless walk.
Names and faces just beyond recall
and a tune with long-forgotten words.
A song of love is a sad song
never more so than when sung
in the halfway mirrored hall
that lies between dreaming and death.

Which is where he lies now
neither dreaming, nor yet dying.
His sightless eyes are mute
his remit to lie still and listen
listen to the sad song of love
from deep within his head
and from a past no longer his.
He drowns in his own lost time
sinking gently beneath the surface
peaceful as a weighted corpse
drifting silently ever downwards
to rejoin the friends of childhood
long gone into that mirrored hall
from which there is no return
somewhere beyond the deepest sleep.

Girl friend at his bedside
softly singing and stroking his hand.

HOTEL WINDOW

During the hours of daylight
all cities are special, and different
but when darkness falls
and the lights begin to burn
they all look much the same.
From behind the curtains
in my high-up hotel bedroom
I looked down on a city
ablaze with noise and movement.
Giant trucks trumpeted angrily
in the gridlocked traffic.
Laundromats and betting shops
were doing steady business
as were the fast food counters
the bars and massage parlours
and the ever-open liquor stores.

Well past midnight now.
Outside it is windy and black
the night sky angry with cloud.
The longer I look the more I see.
The loom of huge buildings
and a tall thin factory chimney
with smoke going straight up.
I see the pale greenish lights
of a sprawling rail junction
scored across by steel lines
hear the wince of a freight train
clanking slowly over points
a reminder that others work
while the city sleeps.
It is all there. Streets, houses,
shops, buses, trees, open spaces
crouched and waiting
hoping to survive the night
and greet the rosy-fingered dawn.

Me too, God willing.

UNKNOWN CITY

I had strayed off route and late at night
found myself on a long road to nowhere.
It was a dimly lit edge-of-city road
of small terraced houses
parked cars and boarded-up shops.
Having nothing to lose
I stopped my car
hoping to find someone to ask
where I was
and more importantly
how to extricate myself
from their unlovely city.
I did not belong there.
I knew it, and they knew it.
They eyed me with the fixed uneasy stare
reserved for the stranger and the alien
since cities began.
Was I muscling for debts?
Peddling insurance?
Or simply calling on the sideline wives
who turned a trick or two
to help the family finances.
Either way, unwelcome.
Beneath a bridge there oozed
a stagnant elbow of canal water
inky and thick as cough medicine.
I avoided two grim looking pubs
heard doleful singing from a gospel hall
passed a school more like a prison
a Chinese restaurant and a garage
before giving up the search
and returning to my car.
At night all cities look alike
and this was no exception.
I could have been anywhere
and felt free to leave
without further enquiry.

HAWK

In the empty spaces between England and Scotland
lies a hideaway hotel with smoke-blackened rafters.
The landlord's wife is a cook of surpassing excellence
grilled trout her special dish.
My bedroom would overlook the fast-flowing stream
where live the plump delicious dappled trout
I hoped to be meeting on my dinner plate
a sprig of commemorative watercress laid alongside.

Somehow I missed the vital turning
and could not find the sequestered moorland hotel
nestling beside its gurgling trouted stream
and knew that I was lost.
Apart from the dismal bleating of sheep
and a bird perched on a rock
there was nothing and no one in sight.
How was it possible, I asked myself,
in such a small and overcrowded island
to be the sole occupant of so much scenery?
I knew then that I would never reach
the snug little hotel with its stone hearth
and blazing boulders of coal
would not sleep on lavender-scented pillows
or tickle the landlady's chin
when her husband's back was turned.
Instead I found that the bird on the rock
was eyeing me with an unblinking stare
that set my nerves atwitch.
It was a hook-beaked bird of prey
sizing up the killing distance
before swooping at me from the rock.

Terrified I drove off at top speed
but it chased the car in hot pursuit.
Daylight fading I neared a town
but could still see in the mirror
the hawk hunting me down.
Sobbing with fright I fled the car
and ran into the safety of a shopping mall.
Even here I did not feel safe
wondering for which past misdemeanours
this bird of ill omen
had been sent to punish me.

COURAGE

For cowardice no cure exists
but the timid and the fearful
have remedies to hand.
They can buy courage in a bottle
or ask for it in their prayers.
Wearing a uniform helps
if not by very much.

Even so the defiance of the timid
is not to be sneezed at.
Dying on your feet
beats living on your knees.
Many a reluctant hero
has been a coward at heart
and thus twice deserving of praise.

Tyrants of the world beware
the anger of the timid man.

ROAD RAGE

Off for a long morning drive
I stab a finger at the radio button
and eagerly await the music
ready to be entranced
exalted
inspired
soothed and made tranquil.

A second later I am spitting blood.
Blood and bile.
Instead of music, an advert!
Dear God, an advert
at just the wrong time
for my fragile state of mind
when I was least disposed to listen
or react sympathetically
to this particular sales pitch.
I was filled instead with an implacable
lifelong iron-fisted resolve
never to purchase the product
being peddled at that moment.
I took its intrusion as a personal slight
depriving me of what I most wanted
and badly needed. Music.
Even my ramshackle old car took offence
and swerved all over the road
provoking angry trumpeting
and headlamp flashing
from the motorised psychopaths
competing for my share of the middle lane.
The huckstering done, surely some music
would mercifully follow, but no, alas no!

Ignoring my fist-shaking snarl of fury
came instead a long insufferable preen
from the presenter, in praise of himself.
How I resented having to listen
to this squirming pimp and defiler
of the living word, a buffoon
with nothing to say
but incapable of keeping quiet.
Just to hear a voice instead of music
was an affront to my frail nervous system
to my digestion, and to my very soul.
Just how much I detested him
at that particular moment
when all I wanted was music
seraphic beautiful music
to beguile and make agreeable my journey
it would be impossible to describe.
One conceited windbag
I might have overlooked but not today.
Today I hated with equal detestation
all his loathsome fraternity
of pestilential radio frontsters
with their jarring bonhomie
their glib offensive put-downs
their patronising small talk
and their insulting references
to me, to us, their elders and betters.
I cursed them all, not once but thrice
from the depths of my bowels.
I swore it, and I meant it.

May they burn in hell for all eternity !

And not just them but their wives
And their children
And their children's children
And their children's children's children
Even unto the third generation.

NIGHT DRIVE IN A BIG NEW MERCEDES

I love to drive at night
love to free my beautiful new car
from the strangled city streets.
Together we seek the open road
eager for the liberating expanse
of the triple-lane freeway.

Then Zoom!

No point in hanging around.
Like an arrow into the fast lane
and speed through the night
relishing the straightline stability
and the silent seamless shutlines
promised in the brochure.
Hauled by the V12 powertrain
I applaud the Stuttgart craftsmen
who make my journey so safe
and so pleasurable
allowing me to possess
those magical hours
between midnight and dawn
when the world sleeps
and I lie cradled
in soft leather cushions
enwombed in the safety
of a massive and beautiful
driving machine
my new S Class Mercedes.
Outside there is strife
everywhere there is chaos
but safely encapsulated
inside my wonderful car
as sumptuously appointed
as an admiral's cabin

I have order and discipline
warmth, darkness and luxury
as I drive on, forever on.

Rain stipples the windshield
but I am snugly cocooned
soothed by the steady swish
and the fat whispering tyres
the wheel peaceful in my hands.
Rendered tranquil by a quintet
Mozart in G Minor softly playing
I slide into a gentle trance
of memories and dreams.

Helped under by the lights
the dimmed hypnotic lights
of my instrument cluster
slow glow-worms in the night
that comfort and befriend me
as I drive on, forever on.
Eyes staring straight ahead
at a million miles of road
seen, unseen and yet to come
riding the wind in the fast lane
to a daybreak far away.

DREAMS

What is youth
but dreams of love?

What is love
but dreams of youth?

What is life
but half-remembered dreams?

What is death
but one long dream without end?

IN PRAISE OF MOTORWAYS

I award First Prize to the designers
and constructors of our motorways
which I regard as industrial sculpture
conceived and executed on heroic scale.
I bestow on them rosettes of gratitude
for carving out their grand design.
Rightly did they ignore the bleating
and whingeing of the fainthearted
as they gouged their carefree way
through the British countryside.

Life for me would be unbearable
denied the pleasure of flowing my car
through the long horizontal curves
and the gentle tilt of the crossfall.
Soothed and comforted
I chart my progress to and fro
on every broad highway in the land
by night as by day
every scarred and ill-lit length
long ago consigned to memory.

Anywhere on the motorways
that food is cooked and sold
I willingly hand over money
and establish customer status.
After a long night drive I pull in
to a welcoming service station
for a comfort break and coffee,
fragrant life-saving coffee.
Then treat myself to breakfast,
full English, a guilty pleasure,
and browse the free newspaper.

Thus relieved, refreshed, replete and better informed
I launch the day.

HIGH HEELS

Corridors were made for high heels
a polished wooden floor
the perfect echo chamber
for this long-striding haughty beauty.
Pointedly she ignores the married men
domestic eunuchs one and all
who eye her in open admiration
as she queens it down the corridor.

No sound arouses male expectation
quite like the sprung rhythm
produced by high heeled shoes.
Heads turn at the fast approach
of these confident bouncy strides
knowing that the legs above the heels
will be driven by long muscular thighs
sheathed in a short tight skirt.

Such frustration, such jealousy!
The married men groan in despair
but cannot avert their envious gaze
nor avoid the stony-faced glare
for those who sneak a backward glance
at the sumptuous hindquarters.
The face says, 'Get lost, you creeps,'
but the strutting swaggering heels say

Look at me! Look at me!

OIL

Ablaze with light, our planet burns.

Even the maddest of emperors
did not squander his patrimony
with such reckless abandon.
Huge buildings hum in the dark
and for every pin-prick in the sky
there is a man-made twinkle
in the sprawling cities below.
Such blinding light, such waste!
We impoverish the planet
even faster than we pollute it
and will have no excuse
if the oil wells finally run dry.

Nothing else works, only oil.
So find us more, search harder
you stinking-rich oil companies.
It is brewed by the hour
in the furnace below our feet
so poke down a longer tube
and suck it up from wherever.
From the ocean deeps
or the sandy wastes
but do not give in, keep trying
until you have found us more oil.

Faith is needed at such times.
Faith in the men with beards
and white laboratory coats
rows of pens in breast pockets
blinking at computer printouts
through rimless spectacles.
Pray for all you are worth that
our mad scientists will find
the way the truth and the light
to keep us in our cars by day
and snug in our beds by night.

Religion does to the brain
what smoking does to the lungs
but don't let that put you off.
Pray, pray, and pray again
that the oil wells never run dry.

DIRTY HANDS

Wealth, all wealth, comes first from dirty hands
busy in the bowels of an abundant planet
mining coal for warmth and gold for wealth
precious stones for the adornment of women
quarrying marble for sculptors to sculpt
snatching pearls from the ocean deeps
and from the sandy wastes and wild shores
black oil, that most treasured of all extractants
for which the planet long ago sold its soul.

Fortunes were made, lost and made again
buying and selling these precious substances
made available to us by a Divine Providence
but which this wasteful planet insanely squanders
and increasingly fights over. Conflict diamonds
weapon grade uranium, we violate the weak
and exploit the impoverished but still fall short
with not enough oil, gas and water to go round
however deep we dig and drill with our dirty hands.

WORK AND PRAYER

Do not be in haste to give up work.
No paid labour demeans a person
and a person at work, any work,
is deserving of respect.

Do not wish for idleness.
Early retirement is slow death.
Work is the only lasting pleasure
and by your work will you be known.

Only fools dream of easy riches.
Legacies bring no luck
and lotteries enrich no one
even those with winning tickets.

Poverty and sloth make cosy bedfellows.
Work and prayer are your stern parents.
Sometimes it is not easy to choose
the path of work and prayer.

Time spent at work is never wasted.
Time spent at prayer is time well spent.
And whether you believe it or not
work can be, and often is, prayer.

SALISBURY CATHEDRAL

750th Anniversary 1258 – 2008

This cathedral was surely never built
by human hand, stone on stone
laboriously hewn and shaped
into existence by mallet and chisel
with sons following fathers
year after slow back-breaking year.
Nor by day labour journeymen
hewing wood for roof timbers
with bells to hang and glass to stain
a vast chaotic building site
a hundred years of unending toil.

Nothing so perfect as this cathedral
could have been fashioned thus.
It can only have materialised
in the manner of all miracles
complete and finished in a day
soaring heavenwards for Evensong
in a great blast of organ music.
Such sublime audacity, such faith!
A sculpted towering masterpiece
witness to the Divine Presence
and the greater glory of us all.

HEAVEN'S GATE

We sorrow for what might have been
We sorrow for all our wasted days
We sorrow for all the wasted love
For the sorrows we could not share
And for the prayers we never said.

Our own sorrow may be hard to bear
Yet we still share a neighbour's pain.
One family will endure in silence
More sorrow than you could bury
In the depths of the darkest coal mine.

If suffering ends at heaven's gate
Let us begin the journey without delay
And direct our footsteps to that end
Where a special place is set aside
For those who weep but cannot pray.

SAINTS AND SINNERS

If to be human is to be divine
and if we are truly made in God's image
then why, in death, is the body of a saintly man
no different from that of a sinner?
And where, among all the blood, fat, sinew and offal
did his immortal soul reside?

HIV POSITIVE

Every time two people have sex
they share their partners of seven years.
All my partners?
And all my partner's partners?
For seven years?
Dear God, have you really been keeping count?
Because if there is a price to pay
for all acts of earthly lust
then I am indeed paying it in full.
If suffering is required of me
for past misdeeds
then vengeance has been exacted
in heaped measure.

Your wrath is terrible, Lord
your punishment swift.
If I am resentful I have good reason
because this unholy pestilence
you have visited on us, your children
is most certainly not a nice way to go.
In fact it is a most unseemly way to go
requiring us to swing a leper's bell
intoning *Unclean! Unclean!*
so the godly may cross to the other side.
I crave the mercy of an easeful death
and a similar dispensation
for all like me, who swing the dreaded bell.

FLU

How is it possible to feel this terrible and still be alive?

It must be flu.
Nothing else makes you so feverishly wretched
shivering one minute
sweating the next
temperature climbing
no appetite whatsoever
sore throat, headache, backache, you name it, it aches.
Classic.
Struggle to bathroom, peer in mirror.
Eyes have a murky yellow tinge.
That's bad.
Search for torch and examine tonsils in mirror.
Just as I thought.
Throat vividly inflamed
a chaplet of rose-shaped pustules ringing my uvula.
Which means I need medication
and must hie me to the surgery with least delay.
Except that I feel too ill to do anything
and so crawl upstairs to bed
gulp a handful of goodnight pills
wash them down with half a bottle of whisky
bandage my eyes against the light
turn the heating up full blast
and sweat it out.

Next year must have the jab.

ALZHEIMERS

Please give my kind regards
to the good Dr Alois Alzheimer
should your paths cross
at some point in the Hereafter.

Tell him his disciples down here
are numbered in their millions
that his name is immortalised
and his fame boundless.

Then ask him why, if he was so clever
he never bothered to find a cure
for the miserable affliction
that will forever bear his name.

LOSING BATTLE

A friend answered me in this way
when asked how he was feeling.
'I'm fighting against time
that's how it is with me.
Fighting against time, as always.'

A battle he was sure to lose
as any fool could have told him.
Because time is the ultimate winner
the strongest force that exists
in this or any other cosmos.

THE SPED ARROW

Surgery is an artisan skill
needing a steady hand
to wield the slotted blade.
The first spurt of blood
the eager rasp of parting flesh
and then the moment of truth.
If the knife does not smart
it does not heal
a due measure of pain
all part of the cure.
A harsh and bitter truth
immutable and ineluctable.
Just as the departing soul
like the sped arrow
and the vanished dream
can never be recalled.

OUR LIVES IN THEIR HANDS

Surgery is an intrusive procedure
the gloved hand and the silvery blade
an unwelcome invasion of privacy.
To be healed by kindly physicians
and their medicine has more appeal.
Hail it as a victory of the intellect
over human frailty and untimely death.

DEATH ON THE TABLE

Too late now to flinch from the box of sharps
the newly slotted blade
the sickly smell
the clink of instruments in dishes
the clump of boots
and the rustle of gowns.

Inert and helpless in this hotel kitchen
white-tiled and stainless-steeled
the cutlery laid out on a dinner trolley
the table set and garnished
with all the shining paraphernalia
of pain, suffering, disease and death.

Blue gowned the anaesthetist
provider of merciful oblivion.
The dangling arm, the gathered vein
the gentlest breaking of the skin
and a last view of the world
beneath the ring of bright lights.

Opening is the easy part.
The surgeon with his supporting cast
of masked and gowned bit players
circle the defenceless body.
Laced with bright arterial blood
the gloved hands begin to maul and palp.

All too soon the first murmurs of disquiet
from beneath the ring of bright lights.
Anxious glances from the scrub nurses
monitors and dials hastily checked
fresh orders issued, instructions shouted
as even the surgeon starts to panic.

But the patient's life gently subsides
and quietly slips away, to everyone's regret.
All that remains is the exit journey
discreetly portered to the basement morgue
a small seemly squeak from rubber tyres
by way of benediction and farewell.

MEDICAL DICTIONARY

Turn first to the entry for Childbirth, Difficulties of
because all life is a journey and it begins here
the start of our contribution to the common weal
our personal dent and mark, our one and only chance
to make a difference, to leave the world
a better place than we found it.

Starkly chiselled prose and intellectual rigour
inform every entry in a medical dictionary.
It is an over-arching summation
a comprehensive overview
of the human predicament.
It lists our body parts item by item
describing first the function of the healthy organ
followed by the malfunction of the unhealthy organ
and then the cure
or lack of cure if none exists.

Once fallen ill we are vulnerable
and act like panic-stricken children
reduced to pleading with intermediaries
those stony-faced and hard-hearted receptionists
who hold the line between us, the sick
and those we beseech with pathetic anxiety
to cure us, to make us well again,
to make us whole,
to tell us that we are not going to die
or that we will not suffer unduly if we do.

If you are squeamish or have a nervous disposition
if you are faint of heart and scare easily
do not consult a medical dictionary.
Because the bleak honesty you will find there
is disconcerting, since few tell the truth
doctors least of all.
Let us commend them for that.
Spelling out to patients or their carers
the grisly details of a degenerative condition
is not lightly done.

As decent men and women
who can blame them for dissembling
when the time comes
as it will to us all
to hear at first hand the dread news
of how much suffering, indignity and pain
will precede our closure.
Because death when it comes
even an easeful death
is a life ended and a flame, however dim,
extinguished, a candle never to be relit.

Our lives zip past at frightening speed
all too soon reaching the chill autumn of late middle age
with our modest achievements elbowed aside
as we bid a final farewell to ambition
all usefulness outlived, all future hope denied.

Down and down we go, pursued with indecent haste
by the afflictions of old age.
Our medical dictionary, unsparing as ever
heartlessly chronicles our decline
the arthritic weakening of every joint
the disintegration of our bone structure
the serial failure of our vital organs
and worse, the degeneration of our brains
so that only the very best of luck and money
will spare us the dreaded care home
that last bleak refuge of the demented and dying.

All that remains are the formal obsequies
with customs duly observed, condolences uttered
and family duty done.
Then aaah, the soothing embalming fluid
the cerement cloths
the winding sheet
the peace and quiet of the mortuary drawer
and the entry for Hygienic Disposal of the Dead.

Finito!

MID LIFE CRISIS

My doctor is a man of candour
and has a telling way with words.
He blames my slack tummy muscles
my thinning hair
my weak bladder and my low sperm count
on a lack of self-discipline.

The words, 'Pull yourself together, man,'
were implied rather than spoken
but the censure and the punishment
were swiftly meted out.
'Two miles,' gasped I. 'Two miles!!!
To walk? Every bloody day?'

'Each and every day,' my stern medical man
commanded, unmoved by my tears.
'No booze, no cigars, no late nights
no rich restaurant food, no casual sex
or anything else remotely enjoyable.
That will put the roses back in your cheeks.'

A living death.

EPITAPH DAY

Every new year since birth
we pass the day of our death.
As we leaf through the calendar
we write this date on our letters
we see it written on newspapers
we hear it spoken on the radio
but never know it is the day
destined to be our dying day.

A Poem for St Valentine's Day

CARNAL PLEASURES

The time will come soon enough
when all pleasures cease for good
and our everlasting peace begins
inside a zinc mortuary drawer
there to ponder at our leisure
on sex, old age and other sins.

Until that dread day comes
eat, drink and heartily rejoice
with wine, women and song.
Enjoy as many carnal pleasures
as your dwindling time allows
and die happy in a lover's arms.

Better than eking out a slow death
in some miserable nursing home
all usefulness finally outlived.
At bedtime nothing more exciting
than a lukewarm milky drink
and two dry biscuits on a plate.

THE NIPPER

A man of ninety and his wife
worked a bungalow smallholding
where they kept pigs and chickens.
Not so, was their triumphant cry
'Pigs and chickens keep us!'

And had, from a wedding day
almost seventy years distant
from which may be deduced
there was little they did not know
about pigs and chickens.

Were they alone in this life of toil?
No. They had a son, born into the job
a man for whom pigs and chickens
held no secrets at all.
A caring swineherd.
A curator of happy hens.

I visited and found a family in turmoil.
Disaster! Catastrophe! Ruin!
The ancient couple were inconsolable.
And the reason for this crisis?
Their son had received his badge of shame
his bus pass, indicating pensionable age.
And with it his intention to call it a day
to exchange pigs and chickens
for the pensioner's white cloth cap
and honourable retirement.

He dreamed of coach trips
of walking the dog
a deck chair and back garden sun.
And a man of sixty-plus
after a lifetime of hard work
surely deserves a charabanc trip or two?

Not according to his distraught parents
who, sobbing, greeted me with the words
'You're never going to believe this.
The nipper wants to pack it in!'

IDEAS

Never apologise for an idea.

Ideas are important, they change the way we live.
Whether it is an idea whose time has come
or one strangled at birth
ideas make things happen in the world.

Trouble, mostly.

K 516

Let us give thanks for Mozart
who lived and died so that we
might have music everlasting.
Through the miracle of reincarnation
from wood, wire and dots on a page
the music lives again, and for ever.

The sound flies from the string
and transmutes to gold
between finger and bowing arm.
Music so exquisitely sad
that I weep to think of the sorrow
which caused it to be written thus.

Music which inspires and exalts
conjured into existence
by a poignant and tragic genius.
Where children are being taught
and Mozart is being played
there dwells the Divine Presence.

K516 is Mozart's string quintet in G Minor

HAMMERKLAVIER

I heard it played in a small salon
this most princely of sonatas
to an audience of serious music lovers
aware of the challenge posed
by this ultimate masterwork.

Sitting near me was a woman
a most handsome older woman
wearing a diamond pendant
that captured the light
with her slightest movement.

At the opening of the adagio
in this sonata to trump all sonatas
there comes a trill
a long slow glittering trill
of the most exquisite anguish.

The diamond pendant
nestling in its luxurious cleavage
picked up the trill
causing it to flash and tremble
in time with the music.

For one heart-stopping nano-second
I shared in the agony of creation
felt the transforming power of genius
learned all I would ever need to know
of life, love, sorrow, death and joy.

*Beethoven's piano sonata Opus 106 in B Flat Major
is known as the 'Hammerklavier'*

MAKING HAY
(Song Lyric)

If you want love
and the perfect mate
don't wait
don't wait
love won't hang around
while you prevaricate.

If love comes your way
don't be blasé
accept at once
brook no delay
cos love won't wait
for ever and a day.

Lovers make haste
don't play about my friend
come quick
come quick
luck needs a helping hand
on that you may depend.

While the sun shines
make hay, make hay.
Love is tempestuous
lovers impetuous
and making love beats making hay
any day.

DON'T GIVE UP THE DAY JOB

What's wrong with a tune you can whistle?
What's wrong with a poem that rhymes?
How plain our language would be
shorn of hyperbole
how dismal verse
if robbed of words all poets love
and pedants scorn
'Lustrous' and 'orotund'
'glister' and 'forlorn'
pearls of our noble English language
cast before those who would deny them
to our aspiring poets
as they rub words together
in the hope of a spark
but I commend them to you
in the belief that poetry is none the worse
for a little judicious embellishment.
and some nice old-fashioned poetic words.

MADE REDUNDANT

How wonderful to be freed
from the bondage of ambition
and the rat race way of life.
Never again the humiliation
of seeking preferment
or the agony of rejection.

Life on the dole isn't so bad.
No more vodkatinis ruining
my digestion. No more hotels,
airport lounges, conferences,
late nights, cancelled flights,
cigarettes or beta blockers.

Only one thing concerns me now.
How soon can I get back?

MIND, BODY AND SOUL

Sooner or later we all fall sick
and thus need to know the secret
the secret that is handed down
from one generation of doctors
to the next.

Priests and physicians
learned this grim secret long ago.
That the malfunctioning body
the hurt mind and the broken spirit
are one and indivisible.

ALWAYS THE WAY

I am a serial questioner
endlessly curious
on matters great and small
although often stumped
for sensible answers.

This is because my father
is no longer around.
He would have known
answers to many questions
I never thought to ask.

PROBUS MAN

I may be a Probus man
but in my soul I am an artist
a dreamer
a weaver of fantasies
a teller of tales
and a great lover.

I may be a Probus man
but I can feel lust.
When my secretary
crosses her black silk knees
and smiles at me
I faint with longing.

I may be a Probus man
but in my soul I am a poet
a dreamer of dreams.
And in those dreams
I square my shoulders
and uncross the black silk knees.

THREE MAGIC WORDS

That open the wallets of married men
hoping and praying the pills will work

Restores youthful vigour!

Beaming middle aged couples
testify that it was money well spent.

MY FRIEND RALPH

I have an admission to make
namely that I am envious
of my friend Ralph, a sales rep.
I envy his big new Beemer
and his gold Amex card
and his air-miles and his tan.
I admire him too
although not as much as I envy him.

Ralph is sleek and well-barbered
fastidiously neat and point-devise.
No grey shows in his hair
even though he, like me,
is now forty, the dreaded forty,
the age which separates
the once and future has-beens
from the permanent no-hopers.

How I wish I could be more like my friend Ralph.

HOROSCOPE

Are we pre-programmed by the stars
or by our genes?
Either way we are dealt the hand
and must play it as best we can.
Do I believe in Fate? Do you?
Shall we say that I am less inclined to disbelieve it
than I once was.

LOVE ME, LOVE MY DOG

Does a dog possess a soul
immortal or otherwise?
It is a matter of some contention.
Assuming that I have one
and may dispose of it as I please
I would willingly share it with my dog.
The companion of every waking hour
and the most trusting of friends.

GIFT WRAPPED

A present is not truly a present
unless the giver suffers a little
by reason of expense
or reluctance
sad at parting with the gift.

If it does not hurt it does not count
so dig deep into the bank balance
put on a smiling face
gift wrap it in kind words
and reap your reward in heaven.

UNHANDY HANDYMAN

My friend Scotty has a limp
from falling off a ladder
my friend Scotty is a finger short
from testing a grain auger
to see if it was working properly.
On both his tattooed arms
he has welding burns
something embedded in an eye
and the scars of many wounds.

At his approach systems malfunction
machines crunch to a halt
and if he touches something
centuries of technology
are powerless to prevent
the havoc that will ensue.
'Bring it round to my workshop'
is Scotty's terrifying battle cry.
'I'll soon have it mended and going again.'

Alas, Scotty cannot be trusted
to measure before cutting
to read an instruction manual
or to put back together
the disembowelled machinery
he has been unable to mend.
So I plead exigency, harden my heart
hire a more competent rival
while trying not to meet his reproachful eye.

This being the eye minus the shrapnel
leaving no doubt that his feelings are hurt
for which I am duly remorseful.
So to ease my guilt
every Christmas without fail
I donate to my unhandy friend Scotty
a bottle of expensive malt whisky
which he somehow manages to open
without the aid of an instruction manual.

UNSKILLED LABOUR

Up with the lark, that's me!

Yes, early rising is great.
The air is so much fresher
the brain is so much clearer
beats me why people lie in
when they could be at work.

Like me, for instance.
Sometimes I've been hard
at it for hours before the
lazy blighters even get up.
No wonder the country etc.

Early to bed suits me fine.
I like my full eight hours.
Longer, if the wife and me
fancy an early night.
Know what I mean!

Soon as my head touches
the pillow, I'm away.
No late nights for me.
I like to wake refreshed
and greet the opal morn.

TAKE A BOW

A soliloquy by Shakespeare
or a sonata by Beethoven
are just squiggles of ink on a page
until liberated by a performer
and transmuted into sound.

The writer and the composer
as primary creators
are dependent on this secondary agent
the re-creator
to conjure their thoughts into life.

However admirable the words on the page
or the notes of music on the stave
if delivered by a mumbling actor
or a banana fingered pianist
they fail.

The genius of creation
relies on this secondary function
the skill of interpretation
and performers by this definition
merit our prolonged applause

Alphabetical List of Poems

Always the Way	94
Alzheimers	81
Autumn	28
Back Benchers	45
Building Site	24
Carnal Pleasures	87
Cheery Chirrup	26
Clockwork Mouse	42
Coastguard Cottage	10
Courage	67
Death on the Table	83
Desecration	19
Dirty Hands	75
Don't Give Up The Day Job	93
Don't Intrude	31
Dreams	71
Drowned Woman	49
Epitaph Day	86
Fidelity	60
First Kiss	55
Flu	80
Gift Wrapped	97
Golden Wedding	56
Good Deed	44
Gravity	17
Hammerklavier	91
Hannibal ad Portas	33
Hawk	66
Heartbreak Planet	20
Heaven's Gate	78
High Heels	73
History on the Big Screen	32
HIV Positive	79
Horoscope	96

Hotel Window	64
How Will It End?	18
Ideas	89
In Praise of Farmers	27
In Praise of Motorways	72
In Praise of Politicians	35
Infidelity	61
Intensive Care	62
K516	90
Lamplight	50
Life Goes On	22
Lingerie	54
Losing Battle	81
Lost Love	51
Love and Toothache	60
Love Cries Out	59
Love Me, Love My Dog	97
Love Won't Wait	61
Made Redundant	93
Making Hay	92
Man of Principle	45
Medical Dictionary	84
Men Best Avoided	46
Mid Life Crisis	86
Mind Body and Soul	94
Motorcyclist in a Coma	63
My Friend Ralph	96
Night Drive in a Big New Mercedes	70
No To Elections	34
Oil	74
Options	39
Ora Pro Nobis	38
Orkney Sky at Night	11
Our Lives in Their Hands	82
Our Lonely Planet	16
Our Wounded Planet	21
Poverty, Piety, Wisdom and Freedom	41

Probus Man	95
Profusion and Disorder	7
Quid Pro Quo	25
Road Rage	68
Saints and Sinners	78
Salesperson's Lament	29
Salisbury Cathedral	77
Second Thoughts	48
Shrubs	12
Sweet Sorrow	54
Take a Bow	100
The Awkward Squad	40
The Dreaded 'S' Word	37
The Many Deaths of a Champion	43
The Nipper	88
The River Stour : Summer afternoon	52
The River Stour : Winter midnight	53
The Sixth Extinction	14
The Sped Arrow	82
Three Magic Words	95
Time	25
Transgression	44
Transience	8
Traveller Tales	30
Unhandy Handyman	98
Unknown City	65
Unskilled Labour	99
Up Close and Personal	58
Volcano	22
Washing Day	9
Why Us?	13
William the Conqueror	36
Wind and Fire	23
Work and Prayer	76

www.ingramcontent.com/pod-product-compliance
Lightning Source LLC
Chambersburg PA
CBHW071308040426
42444CB00009B/1923